D0842809

Letters from God

LETTERS FROM GOD

>>>->>>->>>->>>->>>->>>->>>->>>->>>->>>->>>->>>-<<<-<<<-<<<-<<<-<<<-<<<-<<<-<<<-<<<-<<<

by Frank H. Cheley

>>>->>>->>>->>>->>>->>>->>>->>>->>>->>>->>>->>>-<<<-<<<-<<<-<<<-<<<-<<<-<<<-<<<-<<<-<<<

CHELEY COLORADO CAMPS

ESTES PARK, COLORADO

LETTERS FROM GOD

ISBN 0-9646617-0-5

Made in the United States of America

Foreword

My Grandfather, Frank Cheley, was keenly aware of the many messages we as human beings receive from God. He devoted his life to providing opportunities for young people to get closer to nature to see and appreciate these many messages. My father and mother, Jack and Sis Cheley carried this vision on for another forty years. They planted seeds in young people's minds to encourage them to enthusiastically open up their eyes and take in all that was presented in life. They felt the hurdles we face in our lives were there for a reason. That reason being to make us better people. They took these hurdles to be valuable messages from God.

The presence of Frank's and Jack's messages is very apparent at the Cheley Camps today. Their hope for a better future has become a reality for many because of the great interest they had in young people. A fine summer camp was the perfect outgrowth of such an interest.

The messages within this little book that Frank Cheley conveyed over fifty years ago continue to be relevant today. My wife Carole and I feel fortunate to be able to carry forth the great tradition that Frank started and Jack and Sis continued some 75 years ago. We as human beings sometimes do not want to listen to all of the messages from God. You might consider these as unopened letters. We would all probably benefit from being more receptive to the lessons that are available to us. We know that your mail bag will not only be full but overflowing. Some blank pages were included so you will be able to add many of your own "Letters from God."

Don Cheley
April 1995

Foreword

EVERY boy and girl has at some time felt that they were sick and tired of being " preached at " about religion. Yet every young person has some kind of religion, however hazy it may be, in which he or she believes. All of us go through a stage of wondering just how much to believe of the many things we read and hear pertaining to God and His work. This little book has come into being for just such a purpose; to help you as an individual to learn to recognize all about us the little things that show that God is a real part of every individual and every accomplishment of man.

It is not an attempt to " preach " at you, but is an effort, by a man who lived it himself, to help you to see that a Partnership with God is an essential part of every happy, useful life. It is not a theory or a philosophy that might work, but is the successful formula of one who learned it and used it for greater success and happiness in his own life.

We hope it will help you to find your concept of God adequate for your needs now, today, in today's world, with today's problems.

J. A. C.

Contents

Letters from God

→»» C H A P T E R   I «←

Letters from God

MANY of us at one time or another has asked a trusted friend or adviser an all-important question, "How do you know there is a God?"

Recently a young man put that query to me, and I replied: "What makes you ask the question? Do *you* doubt the existence of God?"

"I have been reading a book," he answered, "that proves conclusively that we cannot know anything about God nor be sure that there is a God. The writer said that, if there is a God, He is outside of the world and of such a nature that we cannot know Him. Is there any way by which we can really *know?*"

"Yes, there is a way to know; there is evidence," I answered. "You recall, I presume, that Robinson Crusoe was dismayed when he discovered that there was another person on the island besides himself. How did he discover it? Did he see any one? No; he discovered *one track of a bare foot in the sand,* and he knew that it could not be his own. He knew that only a human being could have made it, and he knew that whoever had made it could not be far off, for the tide had not yet reached it. All those things he knew to be true, although he had not seen a human being within miles of the island. And that knowledge was all gained from a *mark in the sand*.

" If one print of a bare foot in the sand," I continued, " is absolute proof of the existence and presence of a human being, what are we to suppose when we see the ' prints of the Master's shoe,' as Bunyan calls it, covering the whole wide world? We see a million creatures that only God could make. We see on mountain and in valley the print of the fingers of God. We see a million flowers and plants and trees that only God could make grow. We see all the rivers and the springs of the world fed from the sky. We see a great universe, perfectly made and ordered from the tiniest speck to the greatest of all the worlds. What do all those things mean—those millions upon millions of footprints in the clay of the world? They mean God, living, present, here now and loving! They mean God, my friend, and nothing else."

The young man's face lighted. " I begin to see," he said.

" Moreover," I continued, " we find not only ' prints of the Master's shoe' but we have letters from the Master, from God Himself. I myself have had hundreds of letters from God. Do you doubt that? Let me remind you of the poet's words:

[14]

Letters from God

> " ' There is a book who runs may read;
>   Which heavenly truth imparts,
> And all the lore its scholars need—
>   Clear eyes and Christian hearts.
> The works of God above, below,
>   Within us and around,
> Are pages in that book to show
>   How God Himself is found.'

" Today a grand flotilla of gleaming great airships flew over the city like a magnificent flock of silver white gulls—much too high they were to distinguish any exact details—where they came from we do not know or where they were going we cannot tell—a flotilla of almost mysterious messengers out of the unknown into the somewhere, and as they passed over our quiet peaceful little camp, nestled safely in the everlasting hills, they dropped messages like silver leaves in an autumn breeze and excitedly we rushed to pick them up and read them eagerly, as they fell almost as if they were messages from Mars, and I think we must have felt a good deal as did Walt Whitman when he wrote in his *Leaves of Grass,* referring to the falling autumn leaves: ' I find letters from God dropped in the streets, and every one is signed by God's name, and I leave them where they are, for I know that wheresoe'er I go, others will punctually come forever and forever.' "

" Thank you," said the young man. " I shall be looking for the ' prints ' and the ' letters,' and as I find them I shall realize there is a God." And he left me.

[15]

For him, and other searchers like him, I would tell more about these " letters," and so this little volume is written for it is our earnest conviction that notwithstanding the terrific turmoil and trouble of the present upset and confused world, struggling to achieve a world brotherhood in a newly made world neighborhood, that there is in myriads of individual hearts of all races and all creeds, an ever clarifying hunger to discover and appropriate a God adequate for our times.

To compare the views prevailing today with those of fifty years ago, reveals the fact that youth, both as individuals and as a whole, whether we like it or not, are outgrowing their old concept of a God (who has been to them through the years a glorified person, dispensing reward and punishment) just as our predecessors outgrew the old idea of the Jehovah of the ancient Jews. All of us, whether we know it or not, or whether we confess it or not, in our best moments are unconsciously reaching for a concept of God adequate for our needs now, *today,* in *today's* world, with *today's* problems, right where we are.

We are quite certain that Sam Walter Foss was thinking of modern youth in exactly this connection when he wrote:

> " As wider skies broke on his view,
>   God greatened in his growing mind,
> Each year he dreamed his God anew
> And left his older God behind.
> He saw the boundless scheme dilate

Letters from God

In star and blossom, sky and cloud
And as the Universe grew great
He dreamed for it a greater God."

Obviously it is not God that is changing—it is youth's understanding and ideas that are changing. Youth is inherently religious, deeply genuinely religious—the supreme idealist, yet he is demanding, and rightly so, not a religion of form and ceremony and overly inhibited living of " Thou Shalt Nots." He wants a religion which " is the very warp and woof of common life, one which is the stuff out of which he may weave dreams and hopes and aspirations, one that he may use in all he thinks and does. A mere formal religion of artificial trappings devoid of any power to contribute to human progress will not do."

Modern youth wants a reasonable, scientific religion based upon law which he can understand and use; in which and through which is a God of love and wisdom and intelligence with whom he can team up and pull for better things.

It is because of these deep longings of the heart of youth that the innumerable " letters from God," written about by the poet, have great significance and it is about some of these more obvious " letters " and their meaning that this little volume is written with the hope that discriminating young folks may discover in its brief pages (and appropriate to themselves) some of the inspiring attitude toward life so beautifully expressed by that Sage of Slabsides, John Burroughs, when he wrote:

" The longer I live the more my mind dwells upon the beauty and the wonder of the world. I hardly know which feeling leads, wonderment or admiration.

" I have loved the feel of the grass under my feet, and the sound of the running streams by my side. The hum of the wind in the tree tops has always been good music to me, and the face of the fields has often comforted me more than the faces of men.

" I am in love with this world; by my construction I have nestled lovingly in it. It has been home. It has been my point of outlook into the universe. I have not bruised myself against it, nor tried to use it ignobly. I have tilled its soil, I have gathered its harvests, I have waited upon its seasons, and always have I reaped what I have sown. While I delved, I did not lose sight of the sky overhead. While I gathered its bread and meat for my body, I did not neglect to gather its bread and meat for my soul. I have climbed its mountains, roamed its forests, sailed its waters, crossed its deserts, felt the sting of its frosts, the oppression of its heats, the drench of its rains, the fury of its winds, and always have beauty and joy waited upon my goings and comings."

John Burroughs knew where to find these " letters from God " and how to read them and personalize them to his own good and happiness.

Listen to the further conclusions of another but unknown traveler in pursuit of the great Quest:

" Because I have seen the flowers, I know what color is—what fragrance is—what beauty is.

" Because I have seen the springtime's divine awakening, I know what hope is—what faith is—what joy is.

" Because I have seen the eagle soar and the tall pines swaying in the breeze, I know what grace is.

" Because I have listened to the birds' carol at daybreak, I know what gladness is—what thanksgiving is.

" Because I have seen the seeds reveal their wonders in radiant life, I know what mystery is.

" Because I have looked upon the mountain, the ocean and the trees, I know what majesty is—what grandeur is—what dignity is—what poise is.

" Because I have seen the sun, the moon, and the stars in their ponderous courses, I know what power is, what law is.

" Because God has given us Mothers, I know what faith, hope and charity mean—what understanding is—what forgiveness is; I know what self-sacrifice is—what courage is; I know what undying love is.

" Everywhere in the world about us the Silent Partner, God, has written to us about these things and as I contemplate these kindly simple revelations, my faith mounts to almost understanding."

It is a fantastic thought perhaps, but nevertheless true that away back somewhere in the beginnings of things, even before men had a spoken language at all, the great God-All-Father must have had some way to instruct His children in the basic ways of life. It is quite inconceivable, even with the gift of free choice, that He left them entirely alone to discover through ages of slow experiment by trial and error, the very basic laws upon which their lives must be built in order that they might become happy and useful; so because life was simple and lived in close intimate contact with nature, and because the surest, safest way to teach, even unto this day, is to demonstrate the truth—give it form in life—God deliberately set up for His man-children everywhere and in every phase of life, a great and impressive set of comprehensive Signboards—simple " letters " if you please, each demonstrating a basic principle of right living. Then He equipped His earth people with the marvelous gift of the senses, eyes, ears, a nose and a highly impressionable self-conscious mind, capable of constructive, creative thought so that these helpful " letters " might be persistently contacted and read and understood through the routine of daily living.

As a matter of fact, it is very interesting to note that of all the vast number of things that man believes he has invented and created out of his wisdom, there may be found in nature an exact prototype or " letter from God " forever leading mankind in his search for better things.

Perhaps it never occurred to you, but much of the woodcraft and woodlore of the primitive man was but the learned lessons from the great eternal Signboards and the knowledge and convictions upon which life began were but facts read from God's letters as a result of being constantly thrown in contact with these Infinite demonstrations.

Letters from God

So it is that everywhere in the great out-of-doors, are God's unmistakable letters, as true today as in the very beginning; as fundamental and necessary to usefulness and happiness as they were a million years ago; forming even today the very basis of knowledge and experience, as we shall see as we peruse this little volume together. And even after all these long, rich and wonderful years man, every now and then, is still discovering yet another of God's Signboards, like the laws of radio, always existent but only now discovered, but which have nevertheless tremendously increased our understanding of just how we may tune into and stay tuned into the great Infinite all about us.

These letters seem to be inexhaustible and as man's needs grow and his understanding increases and he is able to raise his conscious awareness to higher and higher levels, lo, there is another Letter from God to meet the condition with God in the lead always anticipating the next step, so that all we need to do is to keep our spirits young and responsive and eager as " little children," in order that we may read as we run, understanding and profiting immeasurably the while.

We are coming to see more and more that there are at the very foundations of life and living, certain great laws; philosophical and ethical conceptions. All real happiness and usefulness are founded upon them. They are never outgrown; they remain constantly through the years our best friends or our worst enemies according as we use them. To go on ignoring these laws in this day spells certain defeat. They are literally the blueprints and specifications for successful, happy living and so simply and so thoroughly are they demonstrated all about us in nature, that none but the veritable " simpleton " can miss them unless he be truly deaf, dumb and blind.

Today we have highly perfected languages, vast libraries of books, in which is the accumulated knowledge and wisdom of all the ages about every conceivable thing, yet God's Signboards upon which He has posted His letters for us have lost none of their significance or importance, for they are entirely free of the usual prejudice or half truth of human opinions. They are God's simple, direct messages to His children and therefore to you and to me.

Often when we do not care to read from man-made books or listen to man-made talk, we like to slip off into the great outdoors and contemplate God's Signboards and gather messages of cheer from them. All one has to do is to go into the big, open spaces with an open heart, an open mind, open eyes and ears and let God be the teacher.

There is no more thrilling outdoor game than seeking and reading these " letters." Have you ever tried to see how many you could find and interpret? Keep a few notes on the way and you will thrill over these " letters from God " just as did Walt Whitman. Here are just a few we have noted as we have traveled the years. May we share them with you?

On Growth

On Growth

ONE of the most sublime facts of life is the fact of growth. *Living things grow.* Where there is life, there is growth. To grow is to ultimately come into your fullest self-realization. Growth suggests *within,* health, vitality, energy in action. Growth is positive. The main purpose of every living thing, therefore, is to grow and unfold after its kind to a logical perfection. Not to grow or to cease growing suggests stagnation, abnormality, retarded development, failure.

All living things grow according to a natural law. Nobody makes them grow because there is an inherent vitality in the seed itself. Humans do not put the self-expansive vitality into the seeds themselves, but we may cultivate the seeds and so " aid and abet " growth.

As a very starting point, God desired that His children catch the significance of growth; that they come to appreciate fully that their main job was to grow and unfold and fulfill their destiny, so everywhere, all about them, He put *growing* things, ever changing, unfolding, developing, which might be observed by all, in fact, growing things which could not be escaped; things growing under all sorts of conditions with an infinite variety of results. Green growing things in good soil and in the open sunshine making big, strong, abiding roots and bringing forth rich fruitage, each after its own kind; and brown lifeless things struggling away in poor soil with all the roots on the surface, battling for life-giving moisture and buffeted by winds and scorching sun; things growing much too thickly, so that each individual tends to be tall and spindly and colorless as they reach skyward for sunshine; blown together in the winds like tall grass and bowed down in multitudes by the heavy storms of adversity. On every hand God provides various conditions of growth demonstrated so that every one of us may see the whole process right before our very own eyes and draw our own conclusions.

You will recall that He put those first two into a garden full of growing things of every sort and description and told them to be fruitful and grow; and in that garden were rich, beautiful, satisfying fruits to feed the life of man and no doubt, some weeds and thistles and burrs of carelessness, thoughtlessness and some sturdy trees that were to grow into great important timbers for significant places—and all were necessary and desirable, each with its special value for the best happiness of the two. *Growth*—what a perfectly marvelous Signboard that is! Surely every one of us will want to read that letter over and over and over again.

On Growth

Or take just trees alone as a Signboard of growth and let us see if we can read the instructions. In the first place, if a tree is to grow large and strong so that it will withstand the heavy snows and terrific winds of adversity, it must grow out in the open. Have you ever noticed a magnificent old maple, hickory or elm standing in the center of a cultivated field, its great branches evenly developed until its crown is a beautiful cone of green loaded with blossoms, then nuts or fruit? The " letter " says, " A tree must have room to grow like that."

In the woods, where they stood thick together, sunlight, moisture and food are scarce and they grow up tall, weak, spindly, each depending on the other for support. Their behavior is like the " mob behavior," because they live in " mobs." While on the other hand, trees in the open always root much deeper, grow much faster and resist disease and decay much better. The " letter " says, " Young folks, get away from the crowd; seek for yourself growing room so that you can become an individual; out where the full glare of the sun can shine upon you; out where the wind and gales can strike you, for only by fighting your way under all sorts of conditions can you hope to develop power and individuality. Get out where you can swing your arms and toss your head; out where you will not be constantly overshadowed by folks not in your class; out where you will have all the chance there is; out where your fruit can ripen and your bark harden and your leaves can give shade and shelter to hot, tired, weary travelers; out where you can mature into a well rounded, capable, competent personality."

Trees are not only letters but whole "books" of useful demonstrated facts. We once camped on the shores of a pretty lake, and just beyond our tent stood a magnificent old oak. How sturdy and strong it seemed to be. How we enjoyed lounging under its great, green arms—and then one night as we slept, there came a heavy storm with much .wind. Suddenly we heard a terrific crack; we bounded out of our cots, and rushing to the flap of our tent, we beheld the old oak prostrate, a great heap of ruins. We could not understand it. We would not have been any more surprised if the sky had fallen in. Taking our little flashlight we hurried to investigate. Imagine our surprise on finding that the entire heart of that old Sentinel had been eaten out by black ants; literally millions of them swarmed out of the huge trunk and scampered all over their victim in wild confusion.

We turned away thoughtfully. The old tree had made such a good appearance. From the outside it impressed one with all that was desirable in a tree, but *inside* all those years it had been entertaining and feeding hordes of black villains, with its very life blood. Then came the unexpected storm—a tragedy, and the inner secrets of a life lay exposed to the world.

The elevators in big department stores flash on white lights when they are going up, and a red one when they are going down. It almost seems a pity that there is not an equally spectacular way of demonstrating the direction in which young people are going, whether they are ascending to new heights of efficiency and self-mastery, like a growing tree, or whether they are dropping into new depths of carelessness and self-indulgence, like a fallen monarch.

Speaking of letters in trees, there is always a postscript on them which says, " Quick maturity; quick decay." As Henry Ward Beecher so well put it, " That which you can grow in a day is lettuce; and how long will it last? That which it takes a hundred years to grow is the oak; and it lasts forever."

We once spent days in the woods with an old forester who was marking ripe trees to be harvested. He would stand back, strike the tree a ringing blow at its butt with a heavy axe and listen. " Sound as a bell," he would say, or " Rotten at the heart," as the case might be.

God's " letters " on growth—have you ever gone to the trouble to read them, or better yet, to study their demonstrated truths? To do so might lead you to a significant discovery about yourself. Try it. You can at least prove your principles.

Are you labeled, " green and growing "? Your whole future depends upon your answer.

On "The Sheer Power of Life"

On "The Sheer Power of Life"

As you have walked through the vast open spaces ablaze with wild flowers or viewed some lovely home yard made beautiful with a riot of color and fragrance, has it ever occurred to you that flowers and trees in bloom everywhere are undoubtedly one of God's most important "letters," saying to all of us who will see, that life is the most majestic fact in the world and that wherever there is life there is unfoldment and promise of greater things yet to be?

This fact was borne home to me one spring day when I was strolling through an apple orchard with the young friend who once had doubted the reality of God. The orchard was at that moment a paradise at high bloom, a perfect bower of blossoms.

"If the trees all *keep their promises,* there will be plenty of apples," I said. "But the apple trees are a good deal like boys, so there may be no apples at all."

" I suppose you mean that a boy is a promise, a promise like the blossoms," laughed my young friend.

" Exactly," I answered. " Frosts nip blossoms and worms eat into promising apples—and boys, too, may never come to fruit. Young human beings, like apples, must pass through a long process of normal growth and development before they reach the richness and beauty of maturity."

" Yes, I know," said my young friend thoughtfully, " and the older I grow the more clearly I see and enjoy this progress from blossom to fruit. Life is truly wonderful."

" And *that* is exactly as it should be," I replied. " It is as God meant it to be or else He would not have planted life so full of intriguing interests nor would He have put us to live in so fascinating a workshop. It was surely meant that humanity should love life—persistent, irrepressible, almost undefeatable life. Humanity was created to live and grow and unfold and come into its destiny."

Life is very much like a spring of fresh water. It simply cannot be repressed nor confined nor held down. It endeavors to flow on and on and on to fulfill its purpose regardless of everything and of anything or anybody.

Henry Ward Beecher once illustrated well this utter exuberance of life:

" When they dug for the Dry Dock in the Navy Yard, they struck a central spring; and the engineer said that it had better have some cement put on it to stop it up. They opened a hole and put in the necessary cement; but the next morning the cement was gone, and the spring was 'blossoming' again. Then the engineer said there had better be some solid rock masonry built in to shut down the spring. So they built it in carefully with heavy stone and reinforcing. The spring waited until they got home and then 'blossomed' out again. They then determined to drive piles deep, deep down, and fix it once and for all. They did drive piles far into the earth, but the irrepressibly alive spring bubbled up again, just as if it did not care one thing about engineers nor engineering. After they had spent some months in trying to stop that living spring, they built a curb around it, and let it run. Vital, flowing life simply could not be repressed. It could be hindered and obstructed but not confined."

So life runs on, forcing itself forever upward, often against staggering odds, until alert, alive, eager folks find the game of living so interesting and so compelling that they live out their busy lives, completing their years doing worth-while things until the event of death and then go on and on and on forever, as " departed heroes," influencing profoundly the lives of those who come after them by what they were.

For ages it has been considered a great honor to die for one's country or for one's ideals or for one's friends. We pay well deserved honor to our martyred heroes, those of long ago and of today. We read their lives and study their achievements with reverence and gratitude for their gifts to us. But we cannot all die for our country. So today we put the emphasis upon *living* as well as upon *dying*. If we live well we shall be able to die well, if the need comes. It is indeed a mighty privilege to *live* for one's country and for one's ideals and for one's friends and for one's God. God needs folks to blossom and grow, to *live* for Him now in a very busy, restless world full of problems.

The unknown poet was thinking exactly these thoughts when he wrote:

> " So he died for his country, that's fine;
> More than most of us do;
> But say, can you add to that line
> That he *lived* for it, too?
>
> *It is easy to die.* Men have died
> For a wish or a whim—
> From bravado or passion or pride;
> Was it harder for him?
>
> But to *live*—every day to live out
> All the truth that he dreamt
> While his friends met his conduct with doubt
> And the world with contempt.
>
> Was it thus that he plodded ahead,
> Never turning aside?
> Then we'll talk of the *life that he lived,*
> Never mind how he died."

So spring, with its wealth of blossoms everywhere,

should suggest life and growth and happiness and usefulness to all of us. Yet so few folks ever really live. They just exist—content to stay in the blossom stage until the petals fall and they are no more.

What do *you* think it means to really live? Some one has put it this way. "To merely exist is to absorb; to live is to give it back again, to radiate." There is the whole wonderful story in a nutshell. It is a scientific fact that the moment a tree for instance stops growing it begins to die, so that living is growing.

But let us be very careful, for so often we associate the idea of growth quite entirely with the visibly physical. Growing does not mean merely adding weight and height and bulk. Growing means development in every phase of our living. There are more kinds of runts than merely physical runts. I know a "six foot sixer, two hundred and fifty pounder" who stands all day pushing a revolving door for folks at a great office building. A little half horse electric motor about as big as a loaf of bread, if properly geared up, could do the job even better.

Physical growth is there but he is a runt mentally and spiritually. His growth was so lopsided that his usefulness is greatly impaired. Normal growth is always well rounded growth. It means a sound mind in a sound body under perfect emotional control. Growth signifies health and strength and courage to live courageously no matter what the "climate." Growth means the thorough development of spirit, mind and body for service—service which will bring about a better world here and now for everybody. Surely that is a challenge to youth!

Living means having the seeing eye, the hearing heart and the thinking hand. Living means being tuned up to the Infinite so definitely that we know we are a part of the great plan and take joy and satisfaction in doing our bit whatever or wherever it may be.

Living consists of discovering for ourselves a rich, satisfying experience in worth-while things well done or as Abraham Lincoln so well put it, " In planting flowers where thistles had grown before." Is that too idealistic to be practical? Not at all. Thousands of great souls scattered all over the earth, of every race and color and belief, have achieved just that. Who is there who will doubt that Dr. Grenfell in his Labrador Wilderness lived a simple adventurous life of service to a simple isolated people? He surely lived. Surely almost above any other living man he has proven that we live most when we give most—that living *is* radiation not absorption but a wise and proper combination of both; inhale, exhale; impress, express. That is living.

There is an old interesting legend that the Queen of Sheba, enamored with the great fame of a certain King, came to visit him, and among the costly gifts she brought was one the King prized above all the rest. It was a beautiful vase filled with a magic elixir, one drop of which would give eternal life and happiness.

The friends of the King heard about the wonderful elixir and when ill sent messengers to him to beg for a drop of his precious fluid. The King, fearing that if the vase were opened its contents would turn to vapor and none would be left for himself, refused all requests. Finally, he himself was taken very ill. When his physicians unsealed the vase, it was empty!

How many lives are empty lives because they fail to blossom and keep growing. After all it is not very involved or difficult to use our talents, whatever they may be, to make all life about us better and finer.

So we find another of God's " letters." Nature abounds with them as says Isaac Watts:

> " Nature with open volume stands
> To spread her Maker's praise abroad,
> And every labor of His hands
> Shows something worthy of a God."

CHAPTER IV

On "Joyous Labor"

On "Joyous Labor"

WE have just been considering what a marvelous thing is growth, but we must not forget that growth comes only with action, at least so far as folks are concerned. To grow we must work; express ourselves. Experience brings growth and experience is what we learn out of what we do. Next to growth, the greatest thing in our lives is creative work.

You recall the old Scripture story that after God placed His first two in a grand and glorious and luxurious garden He told them to prune it and cultivate it and cause it to become productive. He gave mankind the *gift of work* and everywhere on every hand ever since, He has scattered letters endlessly demonstrating the desirability of purposeful, joyous creative labor.

What we use grows. Muscles exercised consistently get stronger and grow more and more capable; talents used expand and unfold into productive skills; minds used develop marvelously; love used returns to us tenfold. Service to others is social-spiritual labor. When we serve we are at our best.

Work is mankind's salvation, for through it he finds self-expression in a thousand ways; he creates into innumerable forms the beauty which he feels in his soul. Every worthy achievement is the result of joyous labor, whether it be a magnificent prelude, a colorful canvas, a well wrought chair, a building, a machine, a character—everything that we achieve is the result of work; a skillful basket; a lovely dress; an appetizing meal; a book; a garden; a worthy thought, all are the product of work. Nothing just happens. And of even more important significance: it is not the products of labor that are the most essential, it is not so important what man makes by joyous labor as it is that joyous labor makes the man, for it is a law of life that we become what we do.

Notwithstanding the fact that many folks are and do become slaves to work largely because of wrong attitudes, fighting it and hating it rather than loving it and welcoming it, yet without work come soft, easy living and decay. We are no longer alert, eager, enthusiastic, challenged, but passive and sedentary and satisfied. The very first thing to do, if you have not already done so, is to fall desperately in love with work, for work, contrary to all too prevalent ideas, is not man's punishment, but his reward, his glory and his pleasure. Only through work do we come into satisfying self-realization. It is very doubtful indeed if there is any happiness without work. We may be more or less successful at amusing ourselves for a time with incidental time-killers but the happy healthful person is the person who has essential, necessary, productive, creative work to do, and if he cannot find it, he must make it. The wrecks of depression were not material; they were spiritual. It was forced idleness that broke men down; not the mere loss of things.

Theodore Roosevelt in his characteristically vigorous fashion declared, " The happiest man is he who has toiled hard and successfully in his life work. The work may be done in a thousand different ways—with brain or hands, in the study, the field or the workshop; if it is honest work, honestly done, and well worth the doing, that is all we have a right to ask."—And Carlyle added, " Blessed is he that has found his work! Let him ask no other blessedness."

As we sat by the dying embers of a camp fire, a thoughtful, wide-eyed boy asked this, " What's God doing now? "

This lad had watched the sun set and the stars come out and the moon come up; about him was a vast panorama of lofty snow-clad peaks and range on range of everlasting hills stretching away to never-land—was it all done then? Was the world a finished job?

And then flashed into my mind this translation of John 5: 17, " My Father is still at work, and I work, too." God is still at work ever improving, enlarging, perfecting. Can you imagine God doing nothing? Perhaps He has only begun some special job and needs your help. Are you willing to help Him?

So you see even God works! His whole creation proves it. Life has meaning and value only as we are able to express our ideas in creative work. Ruskin tells us that " If you want knowledge, you must toil for it; and if pleasure, you must toil for it; toil is a law of life."

And because it is a basic law of all life, God has His Signboards everywhere demonstrating the fact, so that he who runs may read. Every beehive is a Signboard of work, industry and mutual cooperation, for the common good. Sit quietly by an anthill for an hour on a sunny afternoon and see what you can read. Apparently " joyous labor" is the password. Every ant has a job vital to the health and well-being and happiness of the " hill " and he works at it with a will.

Or let's slip over to that placid, lovely pond yonder with the strange little conical roof of aspen branches and clumps of green grass rising out of it, and see one of the most striking Signs of Joyous Labor. We are sitting by a beaver pond; the ingenious dam was built by beavers; the sluiceway at the side to take care of flood waters was built by the beavers. For acres and acres about the pond the young aspen have been cut down, cut into lengths and rolled, some of them five hundred yards, to the pond, by these energetic, enthusiastic, joyous workers—" Busy as· a Beaver," " Working like a Beaver "—by their enthusiastic labors a pond is created which provides an effective moat about their snug, dry home, entered from a hidden under-water doorway.

The pond is their " standing army " and " navy " combined and they toil endlessly, early and late, to keep it in repair, to have a place to store their food and when the pond fills with silt, as it invariably does in time, a new dam is built upon the old. And as one sits quietly in the shadows, we may see a perfect piece of teamwork among the members of the colony—some direct operations; some gnaw down new supplies; some cut it into lengths; some lug it off to the pond, and always all of it in that wonderful spirit of play which makes work joyous, stopping every now and again for a game of tag or a rough and tumble time in the placid waters—no grouches, no grumbles, no long-winded arguments for a six hour day, five days a week—beavers love their work.

Work is the mission of mankind on this earth. Industry is a better horse to ride than genius and much easier to manage. Have you read the " letter " ? It says, plain as day, " To him who will not work, neither shall he eat."

The world is a vast factory, work is its method and civilization is its product! Be glad you can have a little part!

One of our best modern thinkers tells us that " happiness rises out of the joy of self-expression and in creative activity." If you are not happy, then look to your sources. Begin to think creative thoughts, seek creative ideas and impulses; demand opportunities to bring out into form all that you feel yourself to be. In the end you will find that God is seeking self-expression in life, love, wisdom, and form " *in you.*"

Who is there that wants to sit about and do nothing after catching a glimpse of *that* " letter " ? Why, there are not hours enough in a day or days enough in a life to get done all the joyous labor that one wants to accomplish.

On "The Necessity of Training"

On "The Necessity of Training"

Y ES, but you say, " one may work unceasingly forever
and ever and never get to first base. Vast throngs
are mere slaves to their work, driven relentlessly until
they are worn and broken and their spirits soured." True
enough, like all great gifts, even work may be badly
managed. Food is necessary to live, vitality and action
come from food, but one may be a veritable gourmand
and live to eat, instead of eat to live. Love is the great
motive power of the world, the very justification for
existence, yet one may love so consumingly that even
love becomes a selfish gratification. So with work, unless,—and here is another of God's great Signboards,
" To work effectively and joyously and productively,
requires training, education, refining." A slave to work
struggles on blindly, clumsily, ineffectually, blundering
through by sheer physical force, while a joyous, trained
worker finds an easier, more pleasant, more satisfying
way to accomplish good work in less time, so that there

is yet more leisure to study and train and refine one's self.

The more skillful workers do not feel the pressure of slavish toil, for they have trained that inexhaustively competent assistant, the universal subconscious Mind, to be on the job constantly with them. The simple, untrained, primitive man harnessed himself alongside of his patient ox and together they dragged a crude, crooked root through the fields to break up the soil. Untrained man was a mere beast of burden except that potentially he had an objective mind, a self-consciousness which could be taught to think and reason and dream and to consequently turn heavy, exhausting labor into joy and satisfaction.

This same man, trained, enlightened, gathers together in perfectly ingenious ways, from the wide fields of nature's bounty, and by the art of manipulation he produces a hundred horse power tractor which he rides over the fields doing the work of twenty, yes, fifty oxen.

Our whole vast mechanical civilization is fundamentally built on the basic mechanical principles of the lever, the incline plane, and the wheel and the screw. By means of these, in every conceivable combination, man has procured for us civilization and given us, by mechanical improvements, an abundance of things which are necessary to make life more comfortable and livable. By means of applied intelligence (training) man is conquesting the world—and here are the Signs— not a single one of these marvelous mechanical principles was " invented " by man but only discovered by him in nature about him. They are none of them his own inventions. The Great Intelligence has them working in infinite variety in nature all about us. The Indian tradition is to the effect, for instance, that a certain Indian watched a beaver roll his heavy burden easily to the pond, savage man looking on, read the " letter," and conceived the first crude cart with round wheels of log on a crude axle, where for ages before he had dragged his loads on travois. He learned how to trap food instead of running it down, or hunting it with crude weapons. He learned how to make artificial bows and arrows to take the place of the pure physical strength of a hurled javelin. His intelligence prompted him to put " teeth " on his arrows and to add the poison of the snake fang to his artificial mechanical tooth in order to more successfully procure his food.

So, down through countless ages, man, by training himself, has devised new and better tools with which to perfect and simplify work. He has developed himself, if you please, from a cold, half starving savage to a man of marvelous infinite resources and culture. Today we have all about us machine after machine which can almost think, and the end is not yet for there are veritably millions of trained minds working on every problem that faces us and one after another the solutions are found and life in all of its many aspects becomes more and more scientific as man learns to use his infinite possibilities.

Letters from God

Down in the great Texas Panhandle there is enough natural gas coming out of the ground to heat Denver, Omaha, Kansas City, Chicago and St. Louis—think of that! But this gas has to have a pipe to travel in. There must be a channel from the well to the consumer. Men are now stretching great ribbons of twenty inch steel pipe from Texas to Chicago, a thousand miles, to give gas a chance to do the work (and pipes were first demonstrated in nature, river beds, in the stems of plants, in the circulation tubes found in growing trees where sap is pumped all over a tree for its food). So man's self-conscious intelligence, reading God's letters on His Signboards, is applying these demonstrations to his work. Think of it, piping gas and oil all over a vast nation, stopping at nothing, mountain ranges or deserts, to supply civilization with its needs. Without training we might even now be carrying gas and oil in crude containers from place to place by hand!

Virtually all of us have enough talents, potential possibilities, to make a useful living in the world, and education, training, are the tracks upon which we are to get our talents to market. There is no telling in the world what a human, strong of body, trained in mind and relishing the challenge of work, may yet do. It takes time to lay a thousand miles of pipe across a nation; it takes fifteen to twenty years (a third of a life) to get adequate educational tracks laid. Both are absolutely necessary and there are no short cuts. Experience is a good teacher but we have better ways today. So, whenever at all possible, train yourself to do your chosen work easily, effectively, with satisfaction to yourself and others.

Training saves time and effort and doubles up the satisfactions. Put your observations to work as well as your muscles. The Signs say, " Develop your God-given talents! "

And, of course, build where the power is! Make yourself expert at some line of work and then build where the power is.

All of our great cities are built in the locations where power is available for without power to run their industries they cannot exist.

It is the same with a life. It should be built where power is available. You cannot build a successful life on a swamp any more than you can build a successful city on a swamp. You must first locate the source of permanent power and then build your life on that source of power.

We are told that " in Him we live, and move and have our being." There is only one source of power which is permanent enough and strong enough to make it worth while building a life around. The greatest power in the world is the power of God. If you build your life far from this source of power, you build in vain. Build where the power is.

And here is another interesting postscript found on the letter about the necessity for training. It says it is practice which prepares. You see we attempt what in-

terests us, we repeat what satisfies (brings us pleasure).
Satisfied repetition brings skill. In every walk of life
success and usefulness result from endless training and
there are no short cuts! "To him who hath shall be
given and to him who hath not shall be taken away even
that which he hath."

Seek always to be above the average. " General Average " has a great following. Fifty-three percent belong
in his brigades. The mob sets the style in thinking and
acting. Why not belong to the purposeful minority, the
trained few, who can do it better?

A leader is a trained human who can get the crowd
to do what it ought to do.

Every day is pay day for the trained man.

On "Polish Demanded"

On "Polish Demanded"

S PEAKING again of " General Average " and his following, it is interesting to note that the reason so
many folks forever stay " diamonds in the rough " is
because they will not submit to the polishing process—
yet all precious stones are *cut* and *polished* by an involved, intricate treatment which develops their hidden
beauty and brings out, to the very best advantage, their
true luster—all precious jewels are discovered in the
rough. Diamonds are hard, gray, irregular pebbles scattered through common clay and gravel and must be
searched for very diligently. The diamond-bearing earth
is screened and examined minutely on long, endless
belts passing slowly before experts with trained eyes,
and after having been once " discovered " the diamonds
are sorted and sent to the " cutter " who knows just
how to get the very most and the very best out of each
stone in the cutting. The world wants *cut* diamonds,
not diamonds in the rough, no matter what their size.

Beautiful, deep wine-colored garnets are found in stratums of solid granite, high up on rugged peaks, fairly embedded in the rock, much like raisins in a loaf of bread, but they are of no value there. They must be carefully " rescued," and then comes the grinding, polishing process, which is inevitable if they are ever to find themselves in the real market places of the world.

But not only " precious stones " must be polished and refined by extensive experience before they find acceptance and recognition, practically every precious metal has to be smelted in the same way. Have you ever been in a smelter where gold ore is crushed and sifted and separated from baser metal? All sorts of ingenious processes are used to accomplish this refinement. Only very, very rarely is free gold or free silver discovered, and even then in its raw state it is unusable. It must be " melted " and " milled " and " formed " and " fashioned " and " burnished " for its various purposes. Every valuable thing must be " processed " before it comes into its largest usefulness. God has sent many letters proclaiming this fact and has placed innumerable Signs that cry this message to the passing throngs, " *You, too, must be polished.*"

Not only is this great law of life true of precious stones and precious metals but it is as true among practically all foodstuffs and flowers. Isn't it a convincing sign to note that every one of our great variety of luscious fruits, for instance, is but the " polished " off-

spring of simple, more or less useless wild fruit? Think
what has happened to the apple—from a sour, bitter,
tough, wild apple has been developed the Delicious, the
Jonathan, the Rome Beauty, which delight millions.
Think of what Luther Burbank, the plant wizard, accomplished in educating and polishing fruits and grains and
vegetables by the long, tedious process of individual
improvement through endless selection. Today we have
seedless oranges and grapefruit, spineless cactus, white
blackberries and whole gardens full of luxuriant blooms
all polished out of the rough. We have sweet, fat, life-
giving grains, selected and fitted to do their best in
every specialized sort of soil and in every type of climate
by simply bringing to the front the most desirable
qualities and developing each to its own best self-
realization.

Henry Ward Beecher tells us there are a great many
plants which, if you take them in their wild state, show
simply that they have *capacity* and foundation for culture. Some of the choicest of our garden flowers, in
their wild state, were very simple things indeed, in fact
many of them weeds.

Look, for instance, at the gorgeous family of roses.
You will not find in a state of nature roses that parallel
the Teas, the perpetuals and the mosses. These have all
been developed by culture. They have been brought to
a high degree of beauty and fragrance and some to an
excessive degree of fragrance. Is not this another " letter " telling us that it is culture which has made the

[61]

difference, indicating that " folks " can respond to culture just the same as do all other things in Nature?

So Nature's Signboards everywhere about us cry at us insistently—" cultivate," " grind," " polish," " refine," or forever be ignored by progress. Herbert Kaufman tells us that " our value is forever limited unless we have been smelted," and, " that we must stand the cost both in time and sacrifice for the removing of the slag from our minds and from our personalities and from our ideas."

Yes, and we " polish " crude oil into gasoline and naphtha and we polish coal tar into practically all of our vast variety of beautiful dyestuffs and perfumes, so why not polish crude folks to the same fine states of perfection? We " polish " pig iron into hairsprings for fine watches and so the whole vast scheme of polishing and " cutting " and " refining " goes on and on through the medium of wide, rich experience.

Out of tons and tons of pitchblende comes the minutest quantity of radium but with what magical results so that the really significant question becomes, " Just what is the *character* of the material? "

Life is a smelter. Travel and study and all useful activity give each of us contact with men and things and aid in our grinding process, knock off the sharp corners and give us a polish and a luster which greatly increases our usefulness and incidentally our happiness, because as we " improve " ourselves, we find placement, larger recognition, leadership and responsibility.

On " Polish Demanded "

Charles Eliot, perhaps the outstanding of all American educators, tells us that " the fruit of a liberal education [polishing, grinding, refining] is not mere learning, but the *capacity* and *desire* to learn; not mere knowledge but power." And Joseph Addison adds the final touch to the figure by reminding us that " what sculpture is to a block of marble, education worthy of the name [polishing, grinding, refining] is to a human personality."

But we must take the whole matter a step or two further. Polish your personality, of course, but polish your ideas, too! Get rid of your prejudices. They are flaws which greatly reduce your market value. Polish them off. Fine tolerance invariably comes about as the result of much intelligent polishing. Bigoted folks are yet in the raw state. They are all stained up with hate and ill will.

Refine your attitudes which are but your mental habits. Learn to care for people because you come to realize more and more that you are inescapably one with them just as waves are one with the ocean beneath them or raindrops are one with the river into which they flow. Keep open minded. Continually entertain daring, challenging new ideas.

There is scarcely anything that brings the quality of real polish as does consistent creative thinking.

Refine yourself by travel. Go places whenever possible. See things. Do things; explore, investigate.

Read good books continually.

Converse, upon every provocation, with leaders; folks of outstanding achievement. Polish yourself upon them. It will be an even exchange.

There is a whole biography of a certain great leader written in one little significant verse of Scripture. It says, " And he increased in wisdom and in stature and in favor with God and man." That details a comprehensive polishing process. Why not go thou and do likewise?

≫ CHAPTER VII ≪

On "Purposeful Industry"

On "Purposeful Industry"

G ROW and work and develop your latent abilities are basic laws of life demonstrated on every hand by an all-wise Providence, but God's Signboards go farther even than that. They say, plain as day, in addition to the headlines, " Grow, work joyously; be industrious by all means *but always with an objective.*" To merely grow for the sake of growth loses its challenge; to merely labor away in order to have something to do is to miss the great point of industry; to seek development merely to improve your polish and luster is mere vanity *unless it is all to some great end.* There must be an ideal, an all-consuming purpose; a star to which your life is hitched. Ships have ports; shots are aimed at targets; arrows have their mark and lives must have objectives, too, else they become vapid and useless and purposeless. Only those who have a definite port in view and steer straight toward it will ever arrive.

What would you think of an ocean full of neat, trim,

capable boats all just floating around on exhibition? Real ocean-going ships get a cargo and sail for a definite port!

Most folks have only a dim idea of what they want and give no thought to how they are going to get it. They fancy that the tide in their affairs will come to flood some day and bear them on to fortune, but it never does.

One of the greatest forces in life is a "career motive"! which simply means a definitely chosen objective. Successful, happy folks invariably are constantly saying, "This one thing I do. Forgetting the things which are behind, I press forward ——"

It is a tremendously vital and important fact for us all to know, in this very connection, that we accomplish only those things which we persistently image in our hearts. Every great accomplishment is the result of a treasured ideal (a vivid heart picture) which we have not only imagined within us but have contemplated with such persistence and desire that the thing comes to pass, for we very well know that all deeply felt desires tend to externalize themselves, for emotion or feeling is the dynamic of action and when we really feel sufficiently strongly about a matter we usually do something about it and the heart picture becomes a fact in our lives.

First, you see, is born the desire, and as the desire takes definite shape and as we clothe it attractively in our imagination, it urges to action and the first thing we know we are moving toward the realization of our heart picture. The Good Book tells us in very positive language that, " as a man thinketh [feeleth] in his heart so is he." As a man pictures ideals and purposes and objectives deep within himself, so he becomes, for desire stirs to action and we become by doing. The most wonderful part about it all is that so very often when we do get the ideal (the heart picture) actually into action it brings with it a whole vast network of by-products which are extra dividends. That is exactly why nothing succeeds like success, and nothing fails like failure.

Most human failure to achieve can be traced directly to a failure to have a clearly defined objective for without a definite practical objective the whole process becomes wish-thinking, daydreaming, and gets us nowhere. Decide in your mind quite exactly what it is you greatly desire to be or do then picture yourself doing it with such enthusiasm and feeling that you are driven to intelligent action and the whole process gets under way; the pieces begin to assemble themselves and finally by the law of growth you *become*. Nothing on earth can stop you for it is a law of life that your subconscious self gives back to you exactly what you give to it. Life is a vast mirror and reflects back to you exactly what you give it to reflect; if nothing you get nothing back; if a definite something you get a definite something back again.

Sit by any placid pool in the delightful cool of the evening and watch the reflections. They are God's letter on getting back exactly what you give, or drive through any agricultural country and see on every hand the same letter—" as a man soweth so shall he reap." " Do thistles produce figs? " A farmer decides to raise corn so he pictures a corn crop. He plants corn, he cultivates corn and he harvests corn. His objective is to raise corn.

Or let us consider the busy, purposeful, energetic, industrious squirrel, for he is surely an animated letter from God. From crack of day till painted sunset, joyously he seeks nuts, rich pine cones and nut-burrs to store them against a cold winter. In a dozen hollow logs or in high and dry cavities, he stores up nuts and more nuts, a winter food supply, protection for the future, and what chattering, jabbering fun he has doing it, too. Last summer an energetic squirrel adopted a commodious artificial bird house we had put in a great pine tree just outside our mountain cabin. He deliberately gnawed the entrance until he could get his big, saucy, fat self inside with ease and then, believe it or not, he proceeded with much loud talk and endless jabbering, to store that large old roofed-over wooden bucket with a winter supply of nuts. We never were quite sure whether his endless sunrise chatterings were thanks to us for being so thoughtful as to put that lovely little storehouse up for him or whether he was everlastingly scolding us because it wasn't of much larger size, but he filled it full to the door; then he used to sit on the roof and peep in, as much as to say, " There is the realization of a dream of mine. I decided I wanted winter food, and I have it. Let her snow and blow and

what not, I am fixed." And then the *by-product* of that
purposeful industry became apparent. That adventurous
squirrel, in the pursuit of food for *his* storehouse, had
located many, many more rich, seed-laden cones than
he could use and so he set to it burying them, one here
and one there, under the edge of flat stones, in gopher
holes, at the side of rotten logs—*that busy, purposeful
squirrel was planting the future forest and he didn't
know it.* He so loved to work, and his work habits were
so well established that he just felt it his duty to put
safely away every ripe cone he could find regardless of
his own need. We do not know how many storehouses
he had filled but we do know that he was a busy, thrifty,
purposeful " person " and that the world will forever
be the better because of his living.

No man pursues a worthy ideal and brings into
realization a worthy heart picture without scattering
helpfulness all about him. An ambitious boy hungers to
be a great surgeon and as through the years he realizes
his desire, lame walk; blind see; the ill and depressed
smile and take their places again in the army of pro-
ducers. A purposeful girl longs to be a great musician
and as her dream is realized, the very ether waves take
up her melodies and carry them to the ends of the world
to the shut-ins and the downcast and the weary-worn.
She achieves her objective but also brightens many a
corner on the way.

So another of God's letters dropped everywhere says
to all who will read, " Get a worthy objective and de-

vote your very life to its accomplishment with all the feeling and enthusiasm you can possibly muster, and you will find that you come to possess a whole new sense of values; that minutes are precious; that life has flavor and thrill and that there is, after all, great fun in living. Try it."

Keep a purpose behind your industry for in the vernacular of the street, " Pep without purpose is piffle."

CHAPTER VIII

On "Happy Living"

On "Happy Living"

IT is strangely fascinating how these impressive "letters from God" lead logically from one right into another with a perfect sequence almost as if each had a "silver arrow" pointing to the next and so leading us on and on and up and up in our thinking and in our acting; the majesty of growth, the dignity and joy of work that has been trained for until our buried talents are available to ourselves and others; the deep satisfaction of being industrious and making the most of our time and our effort in the accomplishment of our ideals, and now comes along another grand Signboard, which directs folks to happiness.

Whether you have ever thought of it or not, perhaps the deepest hunger of humanity is now and always has been for happiness. From the simple savage in the woodcraft shelter of a tropical island to the most wise and learned doctor in the university, all seek happiness—happiness seems to be the completed puzzle picture and all our efforts and longings and desires are but irregular parts of the perfect picture and successful living is the "art" of putting it all together into a completed whole.

Folks who pursue fame are really hunting happiness. Folks who compromise with loud and lurid notoriety are, deep in their soul, on the trail seeking happiness; folks who are training and putting into practice as best they know their various talents, are all trying to experience happiness. The explorer, the aviator, the artist, the musician, the teacher, the craftsman, the merchant, are all traveling different roads but all are headed for the Capitol of Happiness. Yet, unfortunately, vast throngs are frittering away life's precious hours in trifling amusements and self-indulgence of a thousand varieties with the hardly conscious hope that in some way they do not understand it will all lead to happiness.

More than anything in the world, in our heart of hearts, we wish to experience inward satisfaction and contentment and to feel that we have fulfilled our destiny. They tell us that even the person who gets drunk (poor deluded mortal) is seeking happiness, but he has had wrong "road information" and that instead of being headed for that "peace which passeth all understanding," he is in reverse gear headed for destruction.

Successful living and the "pursuit of happiness," like all the other fine arts, require a technique, demand a skill. Yet it is a philosophy rather than a method for there is no single highway to happiness. One person finds a way in one direction, another in a totally different direction. The important thing is not a patent way but that we get and keep ourselves headed right. Of this much we can all be agreed, true happiness cannot be bought or bargained for, nor can it be presented by any one to another. To deliberately pursue it is like chasing a gorgeous butterfly through green fields—we catch a glimpse of it ever and anon but just as we think we have captured it, in a flash of color it is gone; but if we will pause long enough in our strenuous pursuit of it to sit quietly, like as not it will quite deliberately settle upon our heads for a little before it drifts on to others and yet others.

Happiness is the twin sister of character, both greatly to be desired but elusive and comes only as a by-product of vigorous, purposeful, objective living. Happiness and character are the fragrance of living. They are that bewitching something which life brings to us when we lose our own selves in being and doing our best. Happiness is to living what harmony is to music and what color is to art.

Did you ever notice that when folks are consumed with useful, creative, purposeful work *which they love,* they sing, their faces shine, their voices are soft and friendly? They seem to rise above the purely physical and become strangely spiritual. When they are at their very best, free from all ulterior motive and are just putting all they have into the work in hand, then " that something " steals over them and settles upon them and for an hour they are as happy as children at play.

We watched a busy stonecutter toiling away on a great slab of stone, the great beads of perspiration dripping from his furrowed brow, his hands horny with rough labor; as he deftly wielded his tools he sang, *all day he sang.* We finally asked him what he was doing. He looked at us in great surprise that we should be so ignorant. " Why *I'm* building a cathedral," he said. He had found happiness.

And God's letters on how to be happy while living— they are everywhere in nature. The happy incessant chatter of the busy squirrel planting the forest which is to be; the marvelous song of a myriad of birds as they build their nests and seek for food and lay their eggs and rear their young, and save our crops from insects and our trees from the destruction of wood borers—each living a vigorous, busy, purposeful life, and stopping every little bit to burst into song with the sheer joy of it all, voicing their appreciation for the chance that is theirs, reveling in the sunshine and the wood smells and the murmur of breezes in the tree tops.

Carrie Jacobs Bond sums it all up perfectly in her little verse of gratitude, for at the bottom of all true happiness must be an overflowing spirit of appreciation.

> " Dear God, how good You are to me,
> To give me all earth's beauty, free—
> The birds to sing thro' all my life,
> The flowers to bloom on roads of strife;

On "Happy Living"

In hills or field, where I can roam;
A sheltered path that leads me home;
The sky of every shade and hue—
And then, dear Lord, to give me *You!*"

Happiness is an attitude of heart and mind and soul. It is human fragrance and God has written us extensively in nature how to possess it, yet so many of us are blind and go on forever seeking it in our own mistaken ways; thinking we can purchase it or bargain for it or deliberately appropriate it by force and skill.

"No, no," say the "letters." Try to find the fragrance in a rose; try to gather the smell of new mown hay; try to capture the aroma of fresh ripe fruit. It simply cannot be done, for all, like the happiness we so crave to possess, are but the indefinable life essence of rich life unfolding after its kind.

The happy life is the God-centered life, free from worry and anxiety and frustration and defeat. Happiness comes only from a rich, expanding, exploring, service-filled type of living. When God can genuinely express Himself through us unobstructed and unhindered, then happiness comes to us like a drifting fleecy cloud and all is well with the world.

Want to be happy?
It's up to you!

CHAPTER IX

On "He Never Slumbers
Nor Sleeps"

On "He Never Slumbers
Nor Sleeps"

"THAT 'happiness philosophy' is all very well," I
hear you say. "Sounds logical and simple and easy
but where is the constant dynamic, the Source of Power
to keep us going at our best, to come from? " We are in-
spired to be and do our best, we make firm resolve and
set out resolutely, only to stumble and fall; only to err
grievously. We lose our temper; we take little advantage
of others; we act a selfish part; we judge unkindly; we
gossip and think negative thoughts. We accept much
less than our best from ourselves and before the day is
half over, we find ourselves hopelessly entangled in all
sorts of compromises and the bright ideal of the morning tarnished and dulled. Work which should yield
happiness becomes drudgery and we are downcast and
worried and discouraged and disappointed in ourselves;
disillusioned in our friends, and nightfall finds happiness away yonder in the sunset far away from us as
illusive as the fragrance of a new rain.

How many, many times through the years we have *all* had pretty much exactly that experience and how little really simon-pure happiness there is after all. Study the faces about you, talk with folks you meet and pass on the busy highways of life. How few smiles there are; how few radiant personalities; how few contagiously hopeful folk who are sure of themselves. All carry great burdens which weigh them down—*and so very many folks seem to be forever traveling alone.*

Of this fact we are absolutely certain—God never expected any of us to travel *alone,* or to carry our burdens and disappointments or discouragements *alone.* In fact, He never lets us go our way alone only when we deliberately shut and lock the door and insist upon being lonely, solitary, poorly guided travelers. Many of His greatest " letters " to us proclaim that fact forever in every corner of the earth, night and day, as plainly as if He spoke it in our very ears. He has been telling us since time began, " Lo, I am with you always." From the glorious sunrise in the morning with its light and warmth and color, to the sunset in the evening; from the stars of a summer night to the rainbow of the stormy afternoon, in a thousand ways, He reminds us constantly that He is here now, in all, through all, all in all everywhere, always, " nearer than hands or feet," the great Silent Partner, the inexhaustible Power House of Intelligence, Wisdom, Love, always available; literally brooding over us in His eagerness to travel with us and fellowship with us and show us the way. We should all consider that thought a few minutes every day. It would change everything; our whole outlook, our whole experience.

Harvey Peake voices this thought beautifully in his " Rainbows."

> " My heart is glad when I behold
>   A rainbow in the sky.
> It is to me God's promise that
>   He cares for such as I.
>
> " He hangs this beauty in the blue
>   That I may know His love
> Is reaching from the earth below
>   Up to the heaven above.
>
> " The rainbow brings my eyes delight,
>   And to my soul sweet peace,
> While from my heart there comes this thought,
>   ' God's mercies never cease.' "

We need not be discouraged over any obstacle that appears in our path if we but remember that " all things work together for good to them that love God." In any situation, keeping close to the Father is the thing of greater importance. When this is done, the course of events may be depended upon to work toward the end that holds the greatest possible good. Leaving God out of our plans is the surest possible way of increasing the difficulties in our path, but if we keep close to Him we will find troubles strangely smoothed away, or strength given us to bear them.

The very most fatal mistake of life is to persistently ignore that great Signboard. Most misery and failure and loneliness in life grow out of our absolute insistence that we *go it alone*—and what a long, purposeless, burdensome thing life is when we travel it in that state of mind and with that attitude of heart.

We are to grow and to joyously labor; to be purposefully industrious, helping the Creator complete His plan. We are partners in Creation and when that thought takes hold, everything changes; the puzzle pieces fairly rush together and take on meaning and life holds a new challenge and brings a new satisfaction. We are partners with God in evolving His plan for mankind, not mere chips of humanity floating aimlessly about in the great currents and eddies of life,—from nowhere going nowhere—but earthly representatives of a tremendous enterprise which is unfolding and developing just as rapidly as we will allow it to, for our Great Partner reveals Himself and expresses Himself through us. He has no other way. The frank recognition of that fact would entirely change the whole color of most lives and put new meaning into every effort and every experience, and incidentally, automatically settle for a lot of us perplexing questions as to just what enterprises we could and would share and what participations would be quite unworthy of our Partner. Righteousness means " right-use-ness " and unrighteousness means a " wrong-use-

ness," and after all it is " wrong-use-ness " that brings
sad and lonely hearts.

In light of such a thought, all work and effort and
struggle take on a new meaning. With an actual Silent
Partner we can choose to undertake many a job that we
simply could not see through alone and we will constantly seek to make every effort to express our very
best selves.

We like the spirit of the old prospector, child of nature that he was, who lived high on a mountain slope
facing the east. Each day he rose with the sun and going
out to the edge of the mountain, his head bare, he
greeted the sun as evidence of the daily arrival of his
Silent Partner and would say, " Good morning, God,
what are *we* going to do today? " And then as if perfectly understanding, he would take up *his* work for the
day singing as he labored away at his simple task.

See how such an idea glorifies all work. See how such
an idea puts purpose into the everyday routine of life.
See how such an idea carries religion on from Sunday
into Monday and Tuesday and Wednesday and all of
life. See how such an idea enriches every friendship and
every experience and every wish and desire. See how
such an idea makes of every aspiration a prayer.

We know a kindly old lady whose whole life has been
a veritable benediction and when you ask her how she
is getting on she always says with a happy smile,
" *We're* getting on just grand! " She's read God's " letters " and heeds them too! She has taken God at His

word, " Lo, I am with you always, even unto the ends of the earth."

Solomon, wise man that he was, must have read these " letters " over and over again. From them must have come the inspiration for his writings. Did you ever really find the truth and the beauty in the Twenty-third Psalm as it applies to you as a person? Try it now. Say it very slowly and with great feeling. Say it with your heart as well as with your voice. Say it the very first thing when you waken in the morning. Say it the very last thing before you go to sleep. Say it on the street car. Say it as you stand waiting in line for your turn everywhere you find yourself irritated by delay. Say it before your examinations. Say it before you undertake to perform any task which will try you and prove you; before the game, before the sale, before you preside at a meeting.

Tune in with it night and day, anywhere and everywhere. He never slumbers nor sleeps. Put Him to the test.

On "Everywhere Is Law and Order"

On "Everywhere Is Law and Order"

O F course, partners who are successful pull together. It is team play and cooperation which get any job done. Did you ever drive a balky team? We once started on a month's gypsy trip through the Colorado Rockies with a gang of big older boys. We loaded all our food, bedding and tents into a big wagon, prairie schooner fashion, hired a big strong team and set out for the ever-lasting hills in high spirits and full of visions of real adventure—all of which came true with a vengeance. All went perfectly well with us on the flat level country and the wagon, loaded heavily as it was, rolled right along, but when we got off the main highway and came to steep hill after steep hill, that team rebelled; they simply balked. Together they could have taken that loaded wagon anywhere that a wagon can ever get but instead of a steady, even, determined pull, they see-sawed; one pulled, the other backed; then the other would pull and the first one would stand and shake its head without putting forward a particle of effort. After days of battling that obstinate, ornery team, which refused to pull together, we unhitched them; tied them to the back of the wagon; cut ourselves some stout cross poles; hooked on a couple of stout ropes and the twenty of us pulled that old wagon completely over the Front Range of the Colorado Rockies.

Many a person fails because he balks and *not even God can take the load alone*. And of course there are laws of partnership for all. Life is organized on definite laws. All nature is conducted according to natural law. There is a lawful and an unlawful way to do everything. Law is a man's best friend or his worst enemy. Laws are like habits—it is desirable to have them fighting for you instead of against you; marvelous friends, insatiable enemies. They are the essential rules of the game. A good sportsman invariably plays according to the rules; he knows they were made for the *benefit* of the game, not to hinder and ruin it.

God wanted His partners everywhere to fully recognize the inescapable laws of happy living, so He put everywhere in the universe great Signboards, His "letters" about His great basic laws. Sit quietly and look for an hour into a starry night—worlds without end, vast myriads of them like the sands of the sea, yet they move on and on in perfect order—so perfect that man, even with his man-made instruments, can anticipate years in advance just exactly where each one of these

" grains of light " will be in the heavens at a given time. No matter which way we turn, then, we find *life ordered by law.* What could possibly be more fascinating than the reading of God's " letters " written not only in the stars and the vast innumerable universes about us but also in the microscopic cells of our own bodies?

Listen to this:

" Cells are marvelous considered from the standpoint of their activities and their importance to man, but they are perhaps still more marvelous when considered from the standpoint of their own structure; for they are not only so inconceivably small that it would take more than three thousand of them to form a row an inch long, but they are also composite, being made up of other entities infinitely smaller than themselves, known as molecules.

" And these molecules are also complex wholes; they too are composed of entities that are infinitely smaller than themselves and that we know as atoms. Nor does the wonder stop here, for these infinitesimally small atoms are also composite, being made up of particles called electrons, and even these science does not accept as the ultimate unit, which is thought to be pure energy.

" Noting these facts, a clear picture of the process of construction begins to be delineated; particles of energy combine to form electrons; electrons group to make atoms; atoms draw together to form molecules; molecules combine and form cells; cells combine and form the different organs and substances of the body but always and invariably according to law."

Letters from God

Today scientists are telling us that each of these very atoms is a small universe in itself with a nucleus or " sun " at the center, with " planets," or electrons, revolving around it at frightful, inconceivable, but mathematically proved, speeds, trillions of revolutions in a second. Occasionally one of these electrons (" planets ") jumps out of its place in the atomic solar system, to a higher level. It stays up there, according to scientists, about the one hundred millionth part of a second. And during that period of time, it makes millions of revolutions around its central nucleus or sun, all according to absolute law.

Science is now engaged in " disintegrating the atom " by bombardment. To separate those invisible electrons from the central nucleus to which they are attached by electricity's gigantic power is a difficult task. To knock down the greatest skyscraper or fortress in the world would be easy compared with disintegrating one atom, of which you might have a million in the corner of your eye without knowing it.

So you see there is law and order everywhere. It is inescapable. There are laws of light and of sound and the law of gravitation and the law of association, the laws of physics and the laws of chemistry and the laws of radio, the law of love and the law of compensation. We are surrounded by great, beneficent laws which we can absolutely bank upon and it is up to us to study them and observe them and adjust our lives to them in order that we may benefit by them. When we do we are successful and happy. When we do not, we pay the inevitable penalty because of the *law* of cause and effect, yet, " laws are usable to the degree that they are understood and to the extent that we comply with them."

" We can use any law, physical or metaphysical, when we understand the technique required. In our study of chemistry we learned that to accomplish certain ends we had to conform with the laws underlying the science of chemistry. We learned that water was two parts hydrogen and one part oxygen and that to vary these proportions was to produce, not water, but something else. Likewise, a study of the science of agriculture teaches us that a grain of corn laid on a bare rock will not produce a stalk of corn, but that if it is planted in the earth, it will germinate and produce more corn.

" The human mind is more ready to accept the fact of the inexorability of physical law than the fact of the inexorability of metaphysical law. The body must live, and to do so it requires pure water and sufficient food. The will to live is at the root of our willingness to conform to the laws governing the natural world. But the soul must live, too! We disregard spiritual laws not because of an unwillingness to conform to them intelligently, but because their very subtlety often eludes us."

Suppose, for instance, that one man who is convinced that he is somebody in particular decided on a busy down-town street to suddenly ignore the traffic laws set up and evolved for the safety and protection of all, so he steps on the gas and forces his way against traffic. If he himself is not utterly annihilated, entirely innocent parties likely are; much sorrow and suffering and right down unhappiness result from the obstinate, bullheaded, selfish individualism we see all about us which forgets the great Signs—" Order is Heaven's first law."

God is constantly saying to His partners, " Steady, now let's pull together according to the rules of the game. Look about you." See an orderly directed universe everywhere except where man has taken things deliberately into his own hands for his own ends, regardless —wherever that happens in human affairs, there you have a " traffic jam."

God has given us certain abilities and talents, as well as certain limitations and He has a great broad comprehensive plan for our lives in order that we may contribute most to our day and our time and in turn find the largest measure of happiness. By studying ourselves and knowing ourselves better and by studying the great basic rules of the game with the Silent Partner, we are able to so order our lives that we live productively, effectively, happily and successfully.

Stanley writes, " He has achieved success who has lived well, laughed often and loved much; who has gained the respect of intelligent men and the love of little children; who has filled his niche and accomplished his task; who has left the world better than he found it whether by an improved poppy, a perfect poem or a rescued soul; who has never lacked appreciation of earth's beauty or failed to express it; who has looked for the best in others and given the best he had; whose life was an inspiration, whose memory a benediction."

Such a life has taken full cognizance of God's " letters." " Everywhere is law and order and direction,"— such a life has a certain sense of security which others miss.

If you believe it, why not put it into practice?

CHAPTER XI

On "What Habits Do"

On "What Habits Do"

Among all the instructive letters that our Partner has posted everywhere for our help and guidance, none are more obvious than those which demonstrate the power of habit.

A billion years ago a friendly little river hunted its way from the high Rockies to the Gulf of Mexico. In its meandering it wandered over the great colored deserts of the Southwest, cutting a bit of a channel as it went. Then came the usual spring freshet and the wet seasons one after another, each adding water to the river and each flood cutting that river channel deeper and deeper and deeper. Today the Grand Canyon of the Colorado is a stupendous spectacle, one of the wonders of the world, and what is it? A vast rock-walled prison for a little stream which persisted in repeating over and over and over again a certain action, each action making its imprisonment more secure; its slavery more absolute; a river which dug its own rut so that it must forever run in it. So with every river everywhere, each an unmistakable demonstration of what an action often repeated will produce.

Suppose the Colorado River, running on endlessly in its rocky bed, should suddenly decide to change its course. It would take some great cataclysmic upheaval of the continent to accomplish it. True enough we may dam it with great power dams and divert it mechanically into irrigation projects, but *the river, by often repeated action in a given direction, has determined its own destiny.* So far as we are concerned, it will run forever in its habitual way.

Habit is " aptitude from frequent repetition."

How very few of our actions result from actual exertion of our wills or from careful, deliberate choice—a large percent of them from mere momentum in a certain direction led on by certain *attitudes* which we allow to grow within us, generally quite unguided. The law of gravity led the Colorado River to sea level. It had no will, no attitude, no desire, no ambition to go anywhere in particular but the easy unobstructed way, so it followed the line of least resistance by habit into complete slavery and mankind does exactly the same thing over and over and over again. Thus he establishes a character (which originally meant a stamping upon or the etching out of a metal coin) which is typical of him; good, bad or indifferent. " We are what we do, often repeated," reads the letter, so that " character is habit become fixed." Thomas Carlyle tells us positively that " habit is the deepest law of human nature," and the reason is not difficult to understand for habits become a part of our subconscious selves and operate automatically unless side-tracked by a deliberate act of will.

But good habits are just as easily set into operation as bad when our thoughts, our attitudes, and our feelings are right. Feelings are the dynamic of action. We do as we feel, not as we think—usually we do our thinking afterward and try to build up a rational justification for our actions but *as we think in our heart* (feel) so do we, and so, " as a man thinketh in his heart, so is he."

Do anything good or bad often enough and you form a habit. Smile every half hour for a week and you will form a habit of smiling. Growl every few minutes for a week and you will growl on the slightest provocation because the groove is established and the act becomes easier until the subconscious takes it over and makes of it an automatic habit. If you want to be happy and constructive and purposeful, think positive, happy, helpful thoughts and soon the channels of happy, helpful thinking (feeling) will be established and you will be *acting as you feel*. It is the Law. If you doubt it, try it. Put it to a personal test. By thinking of anything completely and long enough, an individual comes to express it. By repeating this expression frequently enough, he forms a habit. So gently do these weak threads of thought or action grip one that he usually does not notice until the habit is formed and is almost too strong to be broken.

Primitive man knew full well that " little bad habits

are like young wildcats," soft, fluffy, purring, apparently harmless, then as they grow older they become harsh and hard and tyrannical, ultimately to rule with all the relentlessness of tyrants and finally tearing out one's vitals with their sharp teeth and claws. So, the " letter " says, " choke a bad habit while it's young."

Or take another illustration:

There is a story told of a smith of the Middle Ages who was taken prisoner and confined in a dungeon. Because of the knowledge his craft had taught him he carefully examined the heavy links that bound him, expecting somewhere to find a flaw that would show a weak place which could be made to yield. But presently he dropped his hands hopelessly. Certain marks told him that the chain was of his own making and it had always been his boast that one of *his* workmanship could not be broken. He was hopelessly bound with the chain of his own making. We always are. The laws of habit decree it to be so.

Yet what an anchor in times of stress are fine habits deliberately made and of all the habits which one might build for himself probably none is so important or beneficial as the habit of positive thinking (feeling). "Rule the negative out," says God's "letter." Negative thoughts breed negative acts; negative acts make negative character; negative character brings ill health, unhappiness, failure. Establish in your life deep channels of positive thinking and the worries and problems of life are solved. Many have proved it. So may you!

On " What Habits Do "

One of our very best modern thinkers puts it this way:
" There seems to be a law, there *is* in fact a law, the
truth and force of which we are, as it were, just beginning to intelligently grasp." It can be stated in this form:
there is something in the universe that responds to brave
intrepid persistent thought. The power that holds and
moves the stars in their courses sustains, illumines and
fights for those who have read aright God's " letters "
everywhere on the power of habit as shown in oft repeated or continuous action and who heed them.

So it is that faith becomes creative because it *is* positive, clear-cut thought, clearly pictured and kept watered
with earnest expectation until it finds expression for
itself in our objective world.

Gradually, more and more folks, the world over, are
reading with new and deeper understanding God's " letters " on habit, which say as plainly as can be, " Get all
your habits of routine living positive and fighting for
you and see how much time and energy one has left for
new adventures in living. Half the struggles of life
are over when right habits are established, releasing one
for many a journey into far countries for thrilling new
experience."

But how about breaking the bad habits that have
already crept in? Must one forever put up with them and
accept them as fate? No indeed! A way exists to break
up almost any habit, although it requires considerable
will power as well as intense interest and loyalty toward
an opposite ideal. Habit breaking is accomplished by

allowing habits to disintegrate by disuse. For example, if one has acquired the habit of being ill-tempered with his friends, has discovered it and wants to break it, he will find it of little use to try to deaden the habit. He must strike out in an entirely different direction, practicing the art of being good company, and persisting in this endeavor until a new habit is acquired.

On "The Business of Little Things"

On "The Business of Little Things"

How often we meet up with some person who is discouraged and distressed and afraid of life. They seem so small and infinitesimal and utterly inconsequential in the vast complex life about them—so small in fact that they come to feel that what they are and what they do cannot possibly make any difference to anything so they go their own sweet way of folly. They have simply not read the " letters " and need to have them brought to their personal attention, especially the ones that cry aloud, " There are no unimportant little things. Size is never a dependable measure. You remember it was a tiny mouse which set the mighty lion free."

There is a very interesting instance in the first chapter of Genesis and much in point. The author has been graphically describing the majesty of the sun and the beauty of the moon and then, suddenly becoming conscious that he has overlooked a very important matter, he adds in a separate sentence as if it had been appended afterward, " And He made the stars also."

Look about you everywhere in nature and you see the Signs clearly posted calling attention to the fact that big things are just little things put together. Go back for instance to the little discussion of how cells are built up and what cells finally become. Without the basic unit nothing could be made whatsoever. It is out of that " letter " that we have gradually, through the years, come to our present attitude toward the sacredness of personality. Society, civilization as we know it, is built up out of the apparently insignificant " littlenesses." Without them the universe would be barren and higher reaches of evolution would be impossible.

Have you never sat at the edge of a glacier high in the everlasting hills and watched the birth of a mighty river? A drop at a time the sun releases water from the edge of the ice field, gravity picks it up and joins it with other drops of water into a tiny trickle; trickles join trickles to make rivulets; rivulets make little creeks and innumerable creeks rush downward to make a mighty river moving steadily toward the sea. No drops of water, no trickles; no trickles, no rivulets; no rivulets, no creeks; no creeks, no rivers; no rivers, no ocean!

No oceans, no oaks, no snowflakes, no glaciers; and so it goes until we catch a vision of the vast significance of little things. Little ideas have always been behind mighty inventions. Watt watched the steam from a crude teakettle and the result was the steam locomotive. Marconi watched the ripples on a pond move out from the point of agitation to the shore and the wireless

On " The Business of Little Things "

was born which led inevitably to the discovery of radio
and the end is not yet. It is said that the buzz of a fly
resulted in a marvelous Mendelssohn creation. Young
Gutenberg dropped a carved letter he had been whit-
tling into his mother's kettle of dye, and in hastily fish-
ing it out before his mother should discover him he
flipped the dye-covered letter out onto the tablecloth
and printing was born. All little apparently non-consequential incidents, yet do not the " letters " say plain as
day—there are no really little things only to those who
are blind and unaware and utterly unimaginative. Sit
down quietly for a half hour and think through your
experience and you will be startled to discover that every
single significant thing that has ever happened to you
or come into your experience sprang from some tiny
apparently unimportant circumstance so that one should
be careful to seek perfection always in little things for
they *are* vitally important.

The great conductor stood before his mighty aggrega-
tion of instruments and called for order. Something was
wrong; his trained ear had told him so. " Where is the
piccolo? " he said. Imagine it! But the little piccolo was
essential to a rounded harmony.

The story is told that upon occasion a great clock
in the tower of an ancient cathedral stopped. The simple
townsfolk were startled. It was a bad omen. The old
sexton climbed to the tower up dust-laden ladders that
had not been climbed in the memory of man and there
in the " works " was lodged a dead locust. Once a

broken cotter pin in a great steel rolling plant brought the entire factory to a shutdown, throwing hundreds of men out of work. A certain French submarine sank to the bottom with her entire crew. A major catastrophe and when the great hulk was raised to the top a tiny pebble was discovered in a valve refusing to allow it to close as it should.

So one might go on forever. A carelessly omitted comma changed the whole meaning of a telegram and a prosperous going concern was thrown into bankruptcy. One little lie in a courtroom convicted an innocent man to death and left a whole family disgraced forever. One little kindness to a needy cripple at the door brought a fortune in land to a totally unsuspecting family.

Yes, one fly has spoiled many a bowl of soup and one bad egg absolutely ruined an " angel food." Water leaking from a faucet in a stream the size of a common pin wastes about 150 gallons a day, engineers of the United States Department of Agriculture found. Even a leak of only one drop a second makes about four gallons a day. This means a lot of water is often wasted when the water supply may be low.

Watch yourself one day and you will see how it is the tiny annoyances, too, and not the big overpowering problems that grow and grow into ferocious things, and threaten our very existence. This fact is aptly illustrated by the old backwoodsman with very heavy overhanging eyebrows and big brass-rimmed spectacles. One day he rushed frantically into his cabin, seized his gun, took aim through a crack in the door at a big tree which stood near, and fired.

" What is it? " whispered his wife, alarmed by his action.

" A wildcat, Sairy, the orneriest lookin' critter you ever saw—and durned if I didn't miss it."

Hastily he reloaded his gun and started to take another shot, when his wife, who had been peering out at the tree, intervened.

" Hold on, Joshua," she cried, " let me look at you! Why, land's sake, it's nothin' but a little bug hangin' on to your eyebrow! "

" The other day we were talking to a manufacturer and he told us a surprising thing. He said that his actual business of manufacturing made him almost no money at all, but that the by-products showed a handsome profit. ' As a matter of fact,' he said, ' all my main manufacturing business is good for is to give a value to my by-products.' The manufacturing had to be done. Without it the side lines could not exist. It is a fine, dignified business, but there is no money in it. It is the little things, almost insignificant, which are making this man a fortune. We tell you this so you will think it over and see if it fits your case. Are you overlooking any by-products? Is there some side line, connected with your life, which you have neglected? We heard, too, that the meat packers out Chicago way make very little money out of selling meat, but make a great deal out of hides and tallow and hoofs and horns. There it is again. This is an age where we can make a great deal out of what folks used to consider worthless and throw away."

Surely enough has been said to fully illustrate the point. All little things are potentially big things. All little thoughts get to be big actions. All little habits are the beginnings of big habits. All little kindnesses make it that much easier for us to love our neighbors as ourselves. All little misunderstandings lead to disagreements and disagreements lead to war. If there were not little uglinesses there would be no battles, so as some unknown poet has put it:

> " It's just the little homely things,
> The unobtrusive, friendly things,
> The ' won't-you-let-me-help-you ' things
> That make our pathway light.
> And it's just the jolly, joking things,
> The ' never-mind-the-trouble ' things,
> The ' laugh-with-me-it's-funny ' things
> That make the world seem bright.
> For all the countless famous things,
> For wondrous record-breaking things,
> Those ' never-can-be-equaled ' things,
> That all the papers cite,
> Are not like little human things,
> The ' just-because-I-like-you ' things
> That make us happy quite.
> So here's to all the little things,
> The ' done-and-then-forgotten ' things,
> Those ' oh-it's-simply-nothing ' things
> That make life worth the fight."
>
> —Author Unknown.

CHAPTER XIII

On "The Good Life"

On "The Good Life"

So we might go on and on seeking out God's "let-ters" and interpreting them. They are everywhere about us, clamoring to be read, each one with some great vital truth for our happiness and usefulness. What a pity to ignore them! Seek them out yourself and study them for just as surely as you do seek them and find them there will be yet others and others forever as Walt Whitman has said, each one bringing a further en-lightening message of God still at work in His world until ultimately you will stumble onto the "Letter of the Good Life"—a stirring message on helpful service to others.

Grow by all means, grow, expand, unfold; love your chosen work; persistently train to make your work ef-fective and satisfying; keep your ideals clearly defined; and put cheer and enthusiasm into all your efforts; con-sult often with your Partner on plans and specifications; keep all of your thinking and desires in tune with the Infinite; strengthen yourself at every turn with good habit assistants and remember that life, like water, to keep fresh and wholesome and life-giving, must be kept moving, for *motion* is another of those basic laws of which God has written so often in His "letters." Everything in the whole vast scheme of things is forever in motion—vibration. Light is vibration. Sound is vibration. Color is vibration. Health is vibration. Power is vibration. Music is vibration. Service to others is vibration.

All about us in a great variety of ways God has demonstrated this great truth. To keep anything you must give it away—motion. A cool, refreshing, life-giving stream hurries down a moss-lined flower garden, blessing everything it touches as it goes on its way; birds come to drink, the mother deer with her fawn steps lightly to the brink and sips with deep satisfaction and all is well all down the line until that little stream empties into an *obstructed* pool which has no outlet. Green slimy moss springs up; a million microscopic villains lurk in every swallow; a sickening odor rises; living water becomes dead, putrid, poison when it stops "giving" of itself. When motion ceases, decay sets in. We simply cannot live unto ourselves. Serve or die, is the law. Make yourself useful to those about you or else you shrivel and shrink into nothingness. What a challenging "letter" is that!

A while ago we visited the great La Brea pits on the outskirts of Los Angeles, stagnant pools of asphalt which through the bygone centuries had trapped hun-

dreds of specimens of those huge, fierce animals of a
past day and preserved them for us to see—the saber
toothed tiger, the mighty boar-like sloth, the huge mas-
todon, great ferocious monsters, and yet today they are
vanished from the earth; huge, powerful, savage beasts
they were and at first thought one would suppose they,
of all animal life, would survive in the great struggle for
existence by their very power to live and smother more
helpless species, but they are gone forever. They were
self-seekers. They devoured everything in their path.
They conceived the green earth and " all that is in it "
was designed for their own selfish pleasure. They grew
to great bulk physically but their consciousness was at
too low a level. Faster moving, more alive tiny creatures
all about them outwitted them and as they became
" stagnant pools of flesh " they passed out of the picture. They had nothing to give to the life about them.
They served in no way. They were consumers. They pro-
duced nothing save fear. They lived unto themselves
alone and if it had not been for the occasional sloughs
which trapped one here and there and saved it, literally
preserved for us, perhaps as another " letter," we would
never know today that they had lived at all.

Contrast with that sluggish, almost unconscious concern, the little Chinese girl seen carrying a very heavy
baby on her back, singing as she went almost staggering
under the heavy load, and when asked if the load was
not too heavy for her, she quickly replied, " Oh, no, he
isn't heavy; you see he's my brother."

Even an ancient Persian proverb out of the long ago has the gist of the whole matter. It says: " Our most valuable possessions are those which can be shared without lessening. Those which when shared multiply."

" All who joy would win, must share it; happiness was born a twin."

Here are very convincing "letters" out of the long ago that tell the selfsame story. Six thousand years ago an Egyptian ruler decided he would make his fame imperishable. He built the pyramids and in so doing enslaved hundreds of thousands of his subjects to work out his pride. In a Paris museum you may see his mummy for twenty-five cents!

Three thousand years ago Rome decided to build so as to completely overshadow the earth for her own glory. The Cæsars with their bloody eagles are mingled with the dust of Europe. All that remains of that mighty self-seeking Empire is a few good roads, one known as the Appian Way, plenty of ruins and a forever eloquent warning to posterity "those who conquer with the sword will perish with the sword."

Forty generations ago there lived in Syria a simple Carpenter who was born into a world of hate and greed and suspicion. His message was so very simple and direct that even today the world hasn't grasped it and we have been content to consume precious time and energy fighting among themselves over non-consequential details *about* Him instead of projecting His mighty revolutionary teaching to a pathetically needful society, lost in dogma and formalism while His essential message to the world goes unheeded.

Listen to His simple message. " He who is greatest among you is servant of all." " Love the Lord thy God with all thy heart and with all thy mind *and thy neighbor as thyself."*

The poet, Oxenham, sums the better philosophy up beautifully in that grand verse of his, " But Once."

" But once I pass this way and then the silent door swings on its hinges, opens, closes and no more I pass this way. So, while I may, with all my might I will essay sweet comfort and delight to all I meet upon the Pilgrim way. For no man travels twice the Great Highway that winds through darkness up to light, through night, to day."

If by fortunate circumstances and your own fine spirit and energy you get on to better advantage than those about you, do not push off too far alone; reach down and help some of the rest up beside you. Life is a game; humanity the team. Seek to be a star player but a star because you serve the team. The Hall of Fame is a lonely place. One of the real tests of a leader is to be able to get the rest to follow you, not to run off in all your shining glory and be a hermit. " Inasmuch as ye have done it unto one of the least of these . . . ye have done it unto me." Life is a trust; you are the steward; so the good life pays!

Keep forever in mind that fanciful yet tremendously true yarn of the rich king, rich from selfish, indulgent living; so rich that not even the wisest doctors could help him a particle and then the court jester offered a suggestion, " Our king is sad and that is why he is ill. He sits too much, his mind filled with dark foreboding thoughts. If we could make him happy again he would get well." So messengers were dispatched all over the kingdom to bring the shirt of a happy man that the king might wear it, for there existed such a superstitious belief. In vain they sought without success until they chanced upon a happy, friendly beggar standing midway in a dangerous stream, stripped to the middle, helping unfortunate travelers across the turbulent tide; happy he was for he sang and laughed as he toiled but alas he was *too poor* to own a shirt.

He listened gravely to the dilemma of the king, then with a resounding laugh he cried, " Go tell your king to forget *his* troubles by sharing the troubles of *others* and he will get well. Tell him that only in *giving is living*."

The good life is the life of unselfish service. God's Signboards everywhere demonstrate it.

Giving is Living! Living is Giving! And that " letter " is marked " Personal." *It is for you!*

On the steps of a public building in Florence, an old, disabled soldier sat playing a violin. By his side stood a faithful dog holding in his mouth the veteran's hat into which, now and then, a passer-by would drop a coin.

Presently a well-dressed man came along, observed

the object of charity, and asked for his violin. Without hesitating the soldier passed it over to the newcomer, who quickly tuned it more perfectly and began to play.

The sight of the distinguished-looking man and his charming music immediately attracted a large gathering. One by one they began to contribute coins for the benefit of the soldier. The hat in the dog's mouth soon became so heavy with coins that the dog began to growl. It was emptied and filled the second time. Then the performer played the national air, returned the violin and disappeared quickly.

One of the company present said: " That was the great Amard Bucher, the world-renowned violinist. He did this for the poor soldier."

Before the gathering dispersed a comfortable sum of money was presented to the soldier. The great violinist, with a little kindly effort, had flooded the soldier's day with sunshine and had grown himself in the doing of this kindly service which had cost him but little.

David Livingstone, when a poor medical student, heard Robert Moffat say in a public address that Africa was the spot in the world where a young man could live adventurously and deeply. Forty years later he was buried in Westminster Abbey because he had been the light-bringer to a whole dark continent. David Livingstone lived!

On "That We All May Be One"

On "That We All May Be One"

O N this little journey together, studying out God's Signboards, we have read His messages everywhere about us—inspiring, stimulating—and we have at last came to know from His many " letters " on the subject, perhaps the greatest single fact in all life—that God is in all and through all, ever present, everywhere, every second, literally inescapable—and so necessarily within US, too, for if God *did not* indwell us there would be at least *some place* in the universe where God was not and therefore He would not and could not be Infinite, which we know Him to be, so that " God in us " is certainly one of the great " letters " we must not miss.

The great Teacher in the long ago saw it and said it. It was the very gist of His message in His day. " For this purpose came I into the world, to proclaim this gospel [good news]," He said. " Of myself I can do nothing." This was the very gist of His whole teaching. " God in us." " It is the Father that worketh *in* me,

He doeth the works." "I and my Father are one."
Wherever He went, whatever He did He took God with
Him. You can explain the great Teacher in no other
way and by the very same token you can never explain
anybody who is fine and big and worthy except to say,
"It is the Father that worketh in him," in whom he lives
and moves and has his very being—for each of us is a
point of self-conscious divine individualization, basically
Godlike. As one keen observer puts it, "When we act
as though we were like God, we can so easily prove
how much like Him we really are."

He has written it to us over and over again in His
"letters." The Great Teacher was reading one of these
"letters" aloud to His followers when He paused by
the roadside where luscious grapes overgrew the fences.
"I am the vine and ye are the branches," He said; "the
branches find their life in the vine and come forth out
of it and out of the branches come the fruit—that ye all
may be one."

Every tree is a "letter" also—vast myriads of leaves,
each alike, so that the tree may be identified by any of
its leaves but each and every leaf individually different
from any other leaf on the whole tree, the tree with
its roots in the Universal Soil, related, through the soil,
to every other growing thing and yet each tree growing
after its kind. Without soil, no trees at all; no trees,
no branches; no branches, no leaves—"that we all
might be one"—partakers of the same essence of
Universal Life. What a message!

On "That We All May Be One"

Or take the "letter" of the waves on the ocean. Each one rises out of the depths and rolls shoreward, individual and different from every other wave but of the same identical stuff—on to its destiny on the shore where it melts again into the Great Water—a wave it is true with its own life to live but always and inevitably rising out of the deep and inevitably returning to the deep and always, every second of its existence, at one with the ocean from which it sprang.

Or take the "letter" of the sponge, an individual form with its own life and purpose, living *in* the water, surrounded *by* the water, saturated *with* water in which it lives and moves and has its being—literally a living cell in the all surrounding utterly inescapable water. God in us!

A certain big boy who had a very perplexing personal problem that troubled him very greatly went to a kindly man whom he had come to have great confidence in, for advice and help. They went for a long walk together in the woods and climbing a hill, came out on an inspiring promontory and sat down on a log. Away into the night they talked the problem out with all of its far-reaching implications. As they rose to go down the trail together the boy said to his friend with deep feeling, " I wish *you* could crawl inside of me and live there all the time. It would be so easy for me to face life bravely with you *inside* to guide me."

" But," said the kindly man, " I, like you, make mistakes and I would not always guide you aright. Wouldn't it be better if some one could crawl inside of you who never makes mistakes and who would *always* guide you aright? "

The boy was thoughtful. "Yes, but who could that be? "

" As a real matter of fact," continued the friend, " you already have that 'Somebody' there. He has always been there, and He will always be there. No mistake you can ever make will ever drive Him out. He is there because you are you and you are you because He is there. ' Behold I stand at the door and knock. If anybody hear my voice and open the door I will come in to him and will sup with him and he with me.'

" You see," said the friend, " it is a promise—a proposition. The choice is up to you. Behind every thought; behind every decision; behind every desire may be a Silent Partner if you really want that it be so. God, the Father, is eager and anxious to be the *inside* Guide who will help on every problem *if you invite Him to do so.*"

Dorothy Hubbard has said it so very nicely. Let us listen to her briefly:

* " We are all too apt to turn to God after the casualty has happened. Many people seek out God in their search for a panacea for their ailment, whether it be illness, poverty, broken friendships, or perhaps the loss of one held dear. While a jolt may push us Godward, there is no need of it coming that way. The most materially

* Used by permission of the author.

happy person in the world may look as easily and as profitably for spiritual happiness. . . . There is only one way, however, to find this higher job, and that is to devote a part of each day to thinking about God, the true source of all good. We may all tap this source and the simplest way is to start the habit of thinking correctly.

" *If you will think of God being with you, you will never be lonely.* There is a vast difference between being lonely and being alone. Some people prefer a more solitary existence. Others want people around them. Whichever way you are constituted, if you have God with you, you will find yourself with sufficient hours alone or surrounded by congenial friends. Since you are an expression of God it is up to you to aim high. This keeping close to God is a process of growth. You grow through practice. The dancer, through daily practice, learns to control her muscles; the musician learns to control his fingers; the real seeker learns to control his thoughts.

" Those few minutes you are waiting for a train, in the crowded car or subway, relax and feel God being with you. I have found that repeating a short Bible verse is helpful during these brief moments. Or, any inspiring thought that appeals to you is a good habit-forming method. It is not hard to think of a person. You are able to visualize any member of your family, or acquaintance, by merely calling him to mind. It is just as simple to call God to mind. You do not visualize the wind and mentally feel its coolness or whatever it may mean to you and you can think of sunlight, and its warmth. So you can think of God. What does God mean to you? God means good, freedom, happiness, peace, plenty, purity, wisdom and many other things. Think upon these during your spare minutes throughout the day and you will know that God is with you.

" As you go through your daily task think of God as being your adviser and consultant. Feel yourself surrounded by love, feel yourself guided by divine wisdom. It will help you in your associations with people, with your shopping, with any business deal you may have. Cultivate right habits of thinking and your life will gradually open up into avenues of hitherto unsuspected beauty and value. . . .

"You do not need a special room for this. You need no materials of any kind, no pen or ink, no desk or chair. There is no expense involved, you need no person's help. You may practice this habit amidst noise and tumult, or in the quiet of uninhabited places, any hour of the day or night. There are hundreds of times during the day when you are not obliged to be talking to any one, when no one is demanding your listening ear. It is the 'waiting' times you must employ to good advantage. Waiting for a train to go, waiting for a train to stop, waiting for the dentist or the dressmaker, waiting for an elevator to go up or down, little moments of enforced idleness. I don't mean for you to go around the city daydreaming. One should give every bit of his attention when crossing the street, for instance, or whenever one's activity and attention are needed. I am only speaking of the waiting moments. To turn these precious non-productive minutes into profit, think about divine love, harmony, peace and all of the many attributes of the Father in whose image and likeness you are made. *Simply take God along.*

" There is a very good expression that one hears often in the West. When a person meets with a westerner's approval, he says of this person that ' he'll do to take along.' If you happen to be an easterner, this is high praise indeed. It means you are accepted as one of them, that you measure up to their standard of what a man or woman should be. If you will experiment a little you will find that God ' will do to take along,' that His presence will bring you more enjoyment than any human presence could possibly do.

" The beauty of these thought exercises is that, if you should lapse a little, you do not have to go looking for God, because He has never left your side. All you need do is to start in where you left off by acknowledging His presence. ' If I ascend up into heaven thou art there: if I make my bed in hell, behold, thou art there. If I take the wings of the morning, and dwell in the uttermost parts of the earth; even there shall thy hand lead me, and thy right hand shall hold me.'

" So, you see, He hasn't been packed away in storage, there is no dusting off, putting on a pedestal and carrying Him away under your arm with apologies for neglect. No, God is ever alive and vital, at your service as it were. Because you shut your eyes when standing in front of a mountain does not remove the mountain. It is there for you to look at as soon as you will your eyes to open again. All you need to do is to accept God, accept His presence and you do this when you think about Him, whenever you say to yourself, ' God is good, God is love, God is the only power, *I am one with that power.*' Just as simple as that. No rules to this game except single purposeness. It is no gamble, no lottery, no sweepstakes, you may always win—if you will take God along."

So it is as Ina Draper DeFoe so well says:

> " God's world holds the sunshine of heaven,
> The beauty of all growing things.
> Your heart, once attuned, you may listen
> To the faint far-off rustle of wings."

So we come back again to exactly the same point at which we started, only we trust with a deeper insight, to Walt Whitman's lines:

" I find ' letters' from God dropped in the streets, and every one is signed by God's name, and I leave them where they are (for others to read), for I know that wheresoe'er I go, others will punctually come forever and forever."

May you continue to read them and heed them is our earnest wish.

On "That We All May Be One"

GOD, WHEN YOU THOUGHT OF A PINE TREE

God, when you thought of a pine tree,
How did you think of a star?
How did you dream of a damson west
Crossed by an inky bar?
How did you think of a clear, brown pool,
Where flocks of shadows are?

God, when you thought of a cobweb,
How did you think of a dew?
How did you know a spider's house
Had spangles bright and new?
How did you know we human folk
Would love them as we do?

God, when you patterned a bird's song,
Flung on a silver string,
How did you know the ecstasy
That crystal call would bring?
How did you think of a bubbling throat
And a darling speckled wing?

God, when you chiseled a raindrop,
How did you think of a stem,
Bearing a lovely satin leaf
To hold a tiny gem?
How did you know a million drops
Would deck the morning's hem?

Why did you mate the moonlit night
With honeysuckle vines?
How did you know Madeira bloom,
Distilled ecstatic wines?

Letters from God

How did you weave the velvet dusk
Where tangled perfumes are?
God, when you thought of a pine tree,
How did you think of a star?

—Author Unknown.

More Letters

More Letters

More Letters

More Letters